A Norther

Leeds Other Pape.
Alternative Press 1974-1994

Chapter 1: Anarchy in the UK 1

Chapter 2: The Commitments 4

Chapter 3: Digging Deeper 8

Chapter 4: I Fought the Law 11

Chapter 5: News From Everywhere 13

Chapter 6: Part of the Union 16

Chapter 7: With a Little Help From Its Friends 18

Chapter 8: Eight Days a Week 21

Chapter 9: Desperately Seeking Readers 23

Chapter 10: Money's Too Tight to Mention 25

Chapter 11: One Step Beyond 28

Chapter 1

Anarchy in the UK

"Leeds Other Paper exists to provide an alternative newspaper in Leeds, ie a newspaper not controlled by big business and other vested interests. It is our intention to support all groups active in industry and elsewhere for greater control of their own lives. The production will be intermittent at first - we are not professionals and we are few in number. We hope to grow, however, into a regular newspaper. If you wish to help in any way - articles, contacts, distribution etc - your assistance will be greatly appreciated."
(LOP no. 1, January 1974)

In the autumn and winter of 1973/4, as the miners geared up to take on Edward Heath, an alternative to the pro-Tory Yorkshire Evening Post was being prepared in Leeds. According to Mat Hill: "We didn't have a media outlet to publicise the things we were involved in or to help people involved in community action or industrial action to make links. None of what we were involved in got coverage from the established press, or else it got hostile coverage."

At the time, Mat was involved in a claimants' union in Leeds. Along with a group of anarchists and libertarians, mostly ex-students, he helped create that outlet by founding Leeds Other Paper - or LOP. A discussion paper for a meeting on 10 September 1973 which decided to go ahead with an alternative newspaper noted: "The precise content is unimportant ... It can be more community based one week, more strike based the second, heralding the revolution the third..." There was plenty of talk. But there was also action.

Some of those involved had helped sell copies of a short-lived predecessor, The Other Paper, which appeared fortnightly from October 1969 to April 1970. Produced by a separate group, The Other Paper had relied on commercial printers, which was expensive and placed limits on what could be printed. The new paper was to have its own means of production, and the necessary £150 was raised by jumble sales, benefits and a levy from supporters of 6p a week. Suggested titles included Leeds Mercury, Leeds Aire, and Soot - before Leeds Other Paper was agreed upon just before publication in January 1974.

The old press they'd bought was installed initially in a friend of a friend's leaky garage in Bramley, where volunteers sometimes had to negotiate several inches of water while getting the paper out. The first issue was produced on portable typewriters in three different houses, and those bits that hadn't dropped off or blown away were transferred to a fourth house where there was a makeshift lightbox to convert the copy into a metal plate ready for printing. By 2am the copy was beneath a television set with someone standing on top of the TV to make it flat!

Leeds Other Paper emerged on 20 January 1974. But although it was a product of the '1968 generation', LOP was very different from the so-called 'underground' magazines like Oz and IT. It aimed at a working class readership and its commitment was to class struggle, informed by feminism and anti-racism, not to the remnants of a hippy drug culture. The first issue - the only broadsheet in the paper's 20 year history - emerged during Heath's three-day-week state of emergency. Declaring itself the 'Leeds libertarian socialist newspaper', and selling at 4p, LOP exclaimed: "Don't let the bastards carve us up."

Some 500 copies of the first issue were printed, which were mainly sold in pubs. If the initial paper was unashamedly propagandistic, the following issues (with the price down to 3p) took a less hectoring tone. Mat: "We didn't want to be a kind of Socialist Worker propaganda paper. It wasn't pretending to be impartial, it was to counteract the existing Establishment propaganda. We saw it as presenting the facts from the point of view of the people involved, for example in a strike, not just from the boss and the union but from the people on the picket line."

None of the group had previous journalistic experience, although some had been involved in producing a duplicated anarchist paper at the University of Leeds. Mat: "It was experience of working to deadlines because it was published weekly. For a while, when the anarchist bookshop was raided by the police, we published it daily!"

With monthly production, and the page size reduced to the A4 it would remain throughout its life, LOP printed about 1,000 copies per issue and slowly began persuading newsagents to take it. Keith, another of the founding group, explains: "We wanted it to be a paper, and you buy papers in newsagents." Other copies were sold through community groups and some trade union branches. "You produced the paper and then went out and flogged it," recalls Mat. "All the buzzwords of the 80s and 90s like marketing, image and SWOT analysis weren't around in those days."

After a few issues the press was moved to the back of a charity shop in Hyde Park, and Mat was rushed to hospital after nearly slicing his hand off on a guillotine blade. It was not the only occasion that blood was mixed with the sweat and tears. Keith was taken to hospital after badly cutting himself while installing a fan in the photographic darkroom he'd built in his cellar. But there was laughter too. Keith: "I remember falling off my stool in hysterics because the whole thing was so funny. There was Mat, Gordon, Alison, Harry doing the cartoons, a really good atmosphere and people were really strong and determined. There was a real buzz going on then. There were also nine local tenants' or community newspapers in Leeds."

But the members of the original group who did the printing gradually grew apart from those devising the paper's content, and eventually they set up a separate enterprise called Leeds Community Press and began charging for the printing of LOP. "It was like workers' control of the printshop, and the paper was a commercial drag on it," says Keith. The breakdown was symbolised when Keith was physically attacked by one of the printers, whereupon another LOP founder Gordon Wilson threw the electricity switch to stop the press running. So, while reluctantly paying Leeds Community Press to print the paper, LOP once again began raising money to buy its own means of production. "Only this time the co-operative would remain in control so that nobody could take it away," adds Keith.

In 1976 Keith became LOP's first paid worker, at £15 a week. He'd been forced to sign off from Social security when snoopers staked out his house to discover why so many people were coming and going - they were LOP volunteers using the darkroom. The paper went fortnightly in April 1976, a formal workers' co-operative was formed under the name Leeds Alternative Publications Ltd, and in 1978 the Government's Job Creation Scheme was used to add two more paid workers as LOP went from strength to strength. No longer specifically anarchist, it was an independent paper with a left-of-centre editorial line and a commitment to telling it like it was.

LOP became weekly in 1980, and there was an expansion of the workforce when the co-op got its own press again. The co-op ran a printing and typesetting business to subsidise the paper. But eventually both the political and economic tide went out. Renamed Northern Star (after a 19th century equivalent), the paper died 20 years after it began, with sales never rising much above 2,500.

But for two decades Leeds had another voice. According to Radio Four's Wilko's Weekly, LOP was: "A parish magazine of the Leeds dispossessed."

Chapter 2
The Commitments

It was while working for an agency on a job for the News Of The World that I was sent to the home of a woman called Rose Towlerton. She couldn't afford the special non-metal glasses she needed, the NHS wouldn't provide them, so she had contacted the NOTW's 'Captain Cash' column which dished out small amounts of money to readers in need. While telling me how she'd never been able to work since her health had been ruined by chronic nickel poisoning at a Wakefield mill, she produced some dog-eared cuttings which gave her case in detail. The cuttings were ten years old, from Leeds Other Paper in 1981. None of the other press had been interested at the time, but LOP gave in-depth coverage to her battle for compensation. Ten years on, the News Of The World coughed up for a new pair of glasses for Rose but only published one sentence about her case. LOP couldn't give her any money, but it was the only paper to treat her with dignity and publicise her grievances.

"Rose Towlerton comes out in a severe rash and sores whenever she touches anything metallic. She can't open doors, grab a hand rail on a bus, hold a knife and fork, and she has to wear a bra with plastic fasteners. Rose Towlerton suffers from chronic nickel poisoning after working at a Yorkshire mill. She now lives at a homeless hostel in Leeds. The firm responsible first sacked Rose, then offered her £250 for ruining her life ... She told LOP: 'It's not the money, it's justice I want....'." *(LOP 199, November 1981.)*

There are hundreds of people like Rose who would have been denied a voice but for the existence of LOP.

LOP's news values always differed from the mainstream press. While the Yorkshire Evening Post was filled with stories from the established news sources - police, fire, courts, council, business - LOP had its own agenda. It looked for stories with an edge to them. According to one internal discussion paper headed 'Views on the news': "Politically, a good story ... is one that reinforces the ability of the mass of people to do things for themselves..."

Those who set up LOP taught themselves reporting and sub-editing skills on the job, just as they did with production and distribution. Keith: "Going out and getting the news was a whole education. I spent a lot of time in Hunslet and Holbeck at one stage, when the motorways went through. Delivering the papers was a slow process because I'd have to stop and have a few cups of tea for an hour or so before I could move on. People from Hunslet at one stage said 'We're having to find things to do in order to keep up with LOP'. That was in the days when they occupied the Housing department. It was vibrant."

"Twenty tenants from Hunslet Grange and several supporters from Chapeltown Heating Action Group, armed with placards and a petition of 500 signatures, marched into the office of the Director of Social Services in Merrion House. They petitioned him to subsidise Hunslet Grange tenants' electricity bills and take action to prevent supplies from being cut off in the winter ... Keith Mollinson, of the Hunslet Grange Heating Action Group, said: 'I hope this will be the start of more co-ordination between the tenants' heating action groups all over Leeds...'." *(LOP 40, October 1976.)*

To LOP, the mainstream media's news agenda was shallow and ignored people's real concerns. Reporters were sent out to 'get a line' on a story and then move on. In contrast, LOP journalists got stuck in and tried to cover stories in depth and in breadth. While standard coverage of industrial disputes concentrated on the personalities of the leaders and the dispute's effects on trade, for example, LOP recorded such events as working class history told from the point of view of the 'ordinary' people taking part. When the 1984/5 miners' strike took place, LOP played a small but recognised role in counterbalancing the overwhelmingly hostile output of the established media, as former worker Julie Thorpe recalls: "It was exciting because it brought a really intimate view of what was happening in the coalfields to the Leeds readership in a way that was different to how the rest of the media was portraying the strike."

Gordon Wilson, who spent much of the strike getting up in the middle of the night to report from picket lines and soup kitchens across Yorkshire, explains: "The mainstream press concentrated on Scargill and what he was doing, but when you went out on picket lines he was rarely mentioned. It was their struggle rather than his. We very rarely dwelt on anything Scargill was saying. We did report on the issues of 'uneconomic' pits and so on, we informed the discussion, we weren't just reporting it as the working class against the State."

Reporters, photographers and TV crews from the mainstream media occasionally suffered abuse or assaults at the hands of striking miners. According to Gordon, whereas most journalists stayed behind police lines, LOP reporters and photographers stood with the strikers. Although they sometimes had to run from the police, they only once had any hassle from the pickets. Gordon: "The strike was obviously being lost at this point, they were burning barricades and there was serious business afoot. Although they had balaclava helmets on, they objected to us taking photographs. But we talked to them and they were okay after that. We always used to take copies of the paper out with us."

During the year after the strike when the rest of the media had lost interest, LOP went out of its way to give extensive coverage to the series of court cases involving striking miners. Keith: "If you wanted to cover that period in any social history, you should root out those old LOPs and read them."

If the miners' strike was a huge collective struggle, LOP always had room for individual stories like Rose Towlerton's. Stories of people up against a bureaucracy like the council, of tenants trying to get their landlord to do the repairs, of Asian families attacked by racist thugs. It also spotted stories before anyone else and made them into running issues, such as nuclear waste and weapons trains passing through Leeds, local police buying plastic bullets, or councillors banning films like 'Life Of Brian' from Leeds cinemas.

A ten week study in 1985 of media coverage of the Chapeltown area of Leeds, where the city's Afro-Caribbean population is centred, found that while the Evening Post only mentioned the area in the context of prostitution, drugs, policing or rioting, LOP covered the following Chapeltown stories: one court case, one Police Community Forum meeting, a new recording studio, the opening of a multi-cultural centre, a local woman's attempt to raise money for her dance training, reviews of cultural events in the area, and an extensive debate on the letters' page about a proposed dance centre in the area.

As the eighties wore on with the Tories still in power, the level of traditional community and union activity that once formed the backbone of the paper's coverage began to decline. New communities emerged to take their place on the pages of LOP, in the campaign against the poll tax, the militant gay response to AIDS, and the growing confidence of Yorkshire's Moslem population. Saeeda Khanum, a LOP reporter in the late 1980s, recalls the paper's coverage of the Bradford campaign against Salman Rushdie's Satanic Verses. "We were in the right place at the right time for the Rushdie book burning story," she says. "As a journalist who was raised as a Moslem, I had access to stuff that I wouldn't have got otherwise. We had a lot of discussion and we put very uncomfortable views across, it was empathetic but critical. In the early days at least, we were setting the agenda on that. The broadcast media came to us for ideas and contacts."

It wasn't all perfect, of course. Obviously LOP made mistakes, sometimes its attempts at sarcasm were wide of the mark, and the content could on occasions infuriate readers and workers alike. When the paper went weekly there were three workers mainly doing news journalism, plus other workers and several unpaid contributors all working on the paper. But the paid hours for journalists declined over the years and the number of unpaid contributors also fell away.

In the hope of boosting circulation above the regular 2,000+ mark by selling more copies outside Leeds, LOP changed its name to Northern Star in 1991. The name came from a Chartist paper which was published in Leeds from 1837 to 1844 by Feargus O'Connor and other radicals. In the nineteenth century, Northern Star's circulation rose to 40,000. But despite the name change and re-design, sales of its twentieth century namesake stuck at around 2,000.

As circulation stagnated, the political and economic recession took its toll on the co-op. Staff became chronically overworked and the news section was gradually downgraded as the paper became more of a What's On Guide with features. According to Geraldine Lowery, who worked on news and typsetting for the paper's final year: "There were big problems with the direction of the magazine. The people we had taken on weren't seeing it as a political thing, they wanted it to be a music magazine. It was a struggle to make sure there was any news in at all. They said it was because of the news that nobody bought it."

But it was because of the news that it had been set up.

Chapter 3
Digging Deeper

Thousands of textile, leather and print workers in Leeds and West Yorkshire are in daily contact with dyes that may cause cancer. The dyes are made by combining the chemical benzidine with various other substances ... Union research officer Pete Booth told LOP: 'You should see the standards of hygiene at some of the places, benzidine dyes on your bloody sandwiches, literally...'." *(LOP 102, April 1979.)*

It began with a dispute at a Leeds chemicals company in the late 1970s. After covering it for LOP, Gordon came across a member of the Cancer Prevention Society who suffered from bladder cancer as a result of working in the dye industry. He was Ted Rushworth, who alerted LOP to a series of documents available only in the United States, which detailed how certain dyes could cause cancer. It touched a long forgotten chord with Gordon, who years before had taken a degree in textile chemistry.

Gordon: "I suddenly realised that something in my misspent education was actually useful, that I was able to grasp the technical side of all sorts of health and safety issues. Although the documentation was available in the States it hadn't been put into news form or related publicly to dyeing chemicals in this country. We alerted the workers."

Gordon's pioneering work on bladder cancer and dyes was later published as a pamphlet by the Cancer Prevention Society, and featured in a Channel 4 film on the subject. It was an example of LOP not just giving a different slant to the news, but actually breaking stories and investigating issues. For most of the media, health and safety was not a story unless there was a dead body.

Some LOP investigations were helped by moles or whistle-blowers, while others were brought about through hard work or occasionally good luck. They included exposing Government plans for nuclear war with a series of bunkers across Yorkshire; publishing the first leaked copy of civil defence pamphlet 'Protect and Survive'; mortgage lenders boycotting certain inner-city areas; land deals involving Freemasons; National Front claims to have built links with black Moslems; Chilean military personnel being secretly trained in Britain; local companies' use of the rightwing vetting agency the Economic League; possible conflicts of interest in a Government-appointed Development Corporation; and the 'radical right' Tory administration in Bradford under Eric Pickles.

The paper's last major investigation was into allegations that hundreds of homes in the Armley area of Leeds had been contaminated by a multinational company, and that Leeds City Council had been implicated in covering up the contamination.

"It is possibly the most serious case of industrial contamination in the country. And if the documentary evidence of a cover-up is proved, Leeds City Council will be shown to have ignored its responsibilities under the Public Health Act to the extent that it created an environmental time bomb, which the residents of Armley now have to defuse."
(Northern Star 795, July 1993.)

As with Gordon's chemicals investigation, much of the material came from documents available in the United States. Quintin Bradley, reporter from 1988 to 1993, explains: "Everybody knew the documents were around, but I was friends with one of the Armley campaign group so I got the lot. I followed up what had happened in the 1970s and 1980s, I did a bit of door knocking and phoning people up, ex-council officers and so on, which nobody else did. The Evening Post wasn't prepared to go into any detail in the story, and the TV was preparing documentaries, so week by week we'd be uncovering things that nobody else would cover for months."

LOP was unusual in that it was often prepared to publish detailed accounts of issues such as the Armley asbestos case even when the material was not covered by legal 'privilege' which allows things said in a courtroom to be reported without fear of libel action. Despite having fewer resources to defend itself against legal action, LOP was invariably more adventurous than the commercial press. In the early 1980s the Leeds inquest into the mysterious death in Saudi Arabia of nurse Helen Smith was covered at length by all the local and national media. But LOP had been covering the details of the case for a long time before, based on hours spent going over it with Helen's Leeds-based father Ron.

Gordon: "Private Eye had been doing quite a bit of stuff before we latched onto it. We contacted Ron Smith and he was highly interested in us because we were willing to print what a lot of papers wouldn't print. We published the conflicting pathologists' reports and all the other dubious things about the case before the inquest occurred. It was really just ourselves and Private Eye. All the other papers tended to concentrate on was the battle over whether there could be an inquest held in this country or not. We gave it the depth and really got into it, we committed ourselves to telling it from Ron's perspective. His voice was going unheard, and part of our responsibility was to make sure that voice was heard."

A book followed, 'Inquest: Helen Smith The Whole Truth?' by Gordon Wilson and Dave Harrison (Methuen, 1983). A couple of years later Gordon met someone who lived in a nearby street who shared his surname: "He said he'd had a lot of telephone calls for a Gordon Wilson but he hadn't known who I was. My home number is not in the directory. One of these calls had been from Saudi Arabia just after the book was published. This could have been someone threatening to do me in, or it could have been someone willing to tell the whole truth. I suppose I'll never know."

Chapter 4

I Fought the Law

There wasn't a car at the LOP office when an anonymous telephone call said that a train carrying nuclear waste was stuck on the line at Holbeck. So Keith grabbed the camera and just ran the mile or so to capture it on film. It was 1981 and for the previous year or so LOP had been highlighting the dangers of nuclear trains regularly passing through built-up areas of Leeds.

Luckily, the train was still there when Keith arrived, and he started taking photographs from a bridge. But he was spotted by the police officers who accompanied the train, and when they charged up the embankment after him he had to take to his heels again. "I was running with the police chasing after me, and as I ran I wound the film back so that I could hide it before they got me. But I outran them."

Keith had other scrapes with the sharp end of the State as he went about his work reporting and taking photographs for LOP. He was assaulted by police at Leeds railway station for taking a picture of a police sniffer dog, and on another occasion was taken in for questioning at the United States' Menwith Hill spy base in North Yorkshire. "They asked me what I thought of assassinating world leaders, and did I have any connections with Eastern Europe," he recalls.

Julie, meanwhile, was arrested while taking photographs of a 'Stop the City' demonstration in Leeds in August 1984. After being held for nine hours, she was convicted in the Magistrates Court of obstructing the highway but was later cleared on appeal. The NUJ paid for her to be represented by top civil liberties barrister Geoffrey Robertson, and the union went on to win her a £2,050 out of court settlement for wrongful arrest and false imprisonment.

The NUJ had earlier come to the paper's aid in a different battle with authority. When LOP started, Leeds City Council refused to recognise it as a newspaper or to provide it with press facilities such as information on committee meetings, agenda papers, reports and press releases. While sympathetic councillors (usually Liberals) passed information to the paper, LOP set up a legal action fund to challenge the council's decision. But it never came to court. In September 1977 the Leeds NUJ branch passed a motion to send letters to the council administration expressing "full support to LOP's right to reports and other materials already afforded to other members of the press." Just two weeks after the NUJ intervention, Tory council leader Irwin Bellow (later Lord Bellwin) informed the union that he had finally instructed council officers to treat LOP like other newspapers.

Although LOP used the threat of legal action to put pressure on the council, the paper was more likely to be on the receiving end of litigation. Like all small publications, LOP never had the money to defend libel actions in court. Factual corrections would happily be published, and the paper's letters page was always open to differing points of view, but over the years several 'victims' of the paper used the libel laws to extract dictated apologies and out-of-court financial settlements that the paper could ill-afford. They included former Labour Council leader George Mudie (now MP for Leeds East), Evening Post journalist John Thorpe, and millionaire Leeds businessman Manny Cussins.

The then chairman of Leeds United football club, Manny Cussins was paid £1,534.70 in damages and costs for two items published in 1982 about his alleged business practices. The articles were described by his lawyers as "complete fiction from start to finish". As with most of the alleged libels, LOP's natural inclination was to fight - but it had neither the evidence nor the money. The money paid to Manny Cussins left a big hole in the paper's finances. But LOP survived because the entire sum was eventually raised through readers' donations and a series of benefit concerts (helped by the paper's good relations with many on the local music scene).

Several years later, a LOP worker with a long memory pinned up an Evening Post placard proclaiming the news of Manny Cussins' death. It remained there until the paper went bust in 1994. It read simply: "Manny Cussins dead."

Chapter 5

News From Everywhere

Called The Other Voice, it was a 12 page A4 paper with an article about the miners' strike on the front page. And it didn't exist. It was just a dummy of what a national alternative paper could be like, and it was produced in April 1984 at a national conference of alternative papers hosted by LOP. The conference was also attended by people from Islington Gutter Press, Sheffield City Issues, Durham Street Press, York Free Press, Shepherds Bush News, Coventry News, Brighton Voice and half a dozen other papers that were still hanging in there, half a decade into Thatcherism.

There had been many more alternative papers in the previous decade. Some pre-dated LOP, while more formed afterwards. By the late 1970s there were at least 80 different local alternative newspapers, mostly monthly and selling below the 1,000 mark on voluntary labour alone. Some achieved much more for a while. The Liverpool Free Press briefly achieved sales of 10,000, while the Rochdale equivalent RAP sold 7,500. There was even an alternative version of the Press Association, with the duplicated People's News Service circulating stories from all the papers.

In addition, there have been two variations on the alternative press theme. One is the West Highland Free Press, a weekly published on the Isle of Skye since 1972 where there was a gap for a traditional local paper. Still going in 1994, it has filled that gap by itself becoming a traditional local paper, with all the columns of births, deaths and marriages that entails. Although as an independently owned title it provides an alternative to the major newspaper publishers in Scotland, to an outsider it does not appear to fit into any standard definition of an alternative newspaper.

The other variation was the short-lived East End News, launched as a weekly in East London in March 1981. It was prompted by the energies of local journalists facing bias and closures at existing papers. Instead of starting small like most other alternative papers,

East End News took the unprecedented step of raising serious capital before launching. It collected £25,000 (some from national trade unions) and its first issue sold 14,000 copies. But the money didn't last, sales slumped to 4,000 after just three months, and closure followed as the whole project rapidly became uneconomic. LOP workers were peeved when the London-centred national media referred to East End News as the first attempt at an alternative weekly newspaper. "What we could have done with that £25,000," was the rather cynical view from 200 miles up the M1, where LOP had gone weekly on a shoestring five months earlier in October 1980.

The 1984 Leeds conference referred to above came up with the following attempt to define the alternative press. "An unambiguous definition of an 'alternative newspaper' is impossible, but there seem to be features common to all of them. They are: local, anti-racist, anti-sexist, politically on the left, overtly rather than covertly political, not produced for profit, editorially free of the influence of advertisers, run on broadly collective principles ... Most alternative newspapers are small, their existence precarious. With one or two notable exceptions their circulations are in the hundreds rather than the thousands. But this tells us nothing about their influence nor their value. As virtually all the mass media are in the political centre or on the right, the voice of the local alternative newspaper is an important counterweight. Small need not mean insignificant."

In the mid-1990s such counterweights to the mainstream media no longer exist. There remain some listings magazines, but even most of these find it hard to survive. London now manages to support just Time Out (the more radical City Limits and other rivals having folded), while Manchester's City Life was bought by the same company that runs the Manchester Evening News - so it can hardly provide much of an alternative to the local media monopoly.

In a useful chapter on the alternative press published in their book 'What News? The Market, Politics and the Local Press' *(Routledge, 1991)*, academics Bob Franklin and David Murphy described some of the pressures working against alternative newspapers' long-term survival. Workers on papers with a printing press which also does commercial work may by choice or necessity drop the loss-making paper to concentrate on more profitable print work. Similarly, papers can lose their most skilled workers because working on the paper has improved their chances of getting other jobs - paid or better paid - or they leave to find a larger audience for their work. Franklin and Murphy also identified an increased reliance on listings as a selling point, and the choice of features increasingly aimed at attracting enough advertisers to maintain income levels. The authors noted that, with the then exception of LOP/Northern Star, radical papers either went under after a few entertaining years, or followed the listings magazine Time Out down the consumerist road of peddling 'style'.

Ironically, the decline of the alternative press and the consequent narrowing of readers' choice coincided with the arrival of new technologies such as desktop publishing which should have made it easier for people to get into print. The same period has also seen new technology (combined with weakening the print unions) fail to deliver the promised increase in the number of national papers. News on Sunday, the Sunday Correspondent and The Post are all long dead, Today is owned by Rupert Murdoch, and the Independent titles have been taken over by the Mirror Group. As independent papers, LOP outlived them all.

Politicians may tell us that 'the market' will provide for all our needs, but market forces have not allowed the continued existence of alternative papers for those of us that want them. As Franklin and Murphy noted: "The alternative radical press do not provide an example of the free market creating choice and variety. Quite the reverse: they show it consuming them."

Chapter 6
Part of the Union

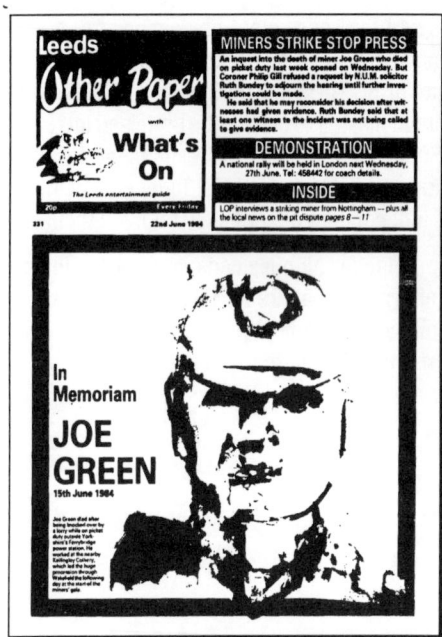

Why should LOP's paid workers be allowed into the same trade union as journalists earning four or five times as much? It was a question which, for a time, perplexed members of the National Union of Journalists in Leeds. As LOP's first paid worker, Keith applied for membership of the NUJ, which was granted with some misgivings: "There was suspicion from most other journalists from the straight media. We were treated as odd, because we didn't dress normally and we didn't behave normally."

Once in the branch, Keith helped improve LOP's standing by taking on the unenviable task of being treasurer of the Leeds branch. "I took it on just to show that LOP workers were willing to take their turn at grotty jobs, there was no glamour to it at all." During the 1978 provincial journalists' national strike, LOP workers helped striking journalists in York produce their own paper.

Despite this and Keith's role as treasurer, the next few LOP reporters who joined the NUJ also faced accusations from some members that they weren't 'proper journalists'. In 1981 the Leeds NUJ branch executive conducted an investigation into wages and conditions at LOP which found that, while wages of £56 a week were well below the Newspaper Society minimum of £82, workers enjoyed other unheard-of benefits such as paternity leave and editorial control of their work. When the report was discussed at a branch meeting in March 1981, a member from the Evening Post said he did not see why such low paid members should have the same voting rights at branch meetings as those earning several times more. He also attacked LOP for its criticisms of other NUJ members in its columns. But LOP was defended by other branch members, and the report was simply noted.

Keith: "I couldn't understand what the problem was. The fact that I was on an abysmal income was quite irrelevant. We were a union, not a management organisation or some poncey professional body. It was interesting that we should be seen as such a threat really, both to the Evening Post and to the union. But we were quite gratified in a way to be seen as so important."

Relations improved and in 1988 the NUJ annual conference collected £181.15 to help LOP survive one of its periodic financial crises.

As an alternative newspaper, LOP saw it as its duty to point out to readers what was wrong with the existing media. Printers' strikes at Yorkshire Post Newspapers would get particularly good coverage, as would profit figures, links between the owners of the Yorkshire Post and Yorkshire Television, and critiques of the media's coverage of big local issues. LOP was particularly critical of the media's coverage of violence against women in the context of the 'Yorkshire Ripper' crimes. Pin-up pictures placed next to reports of rape, and the assumption that women rather than men should be placed under curfew, were also attacked in the columns of LOP. And in May 1981 LOP revealed in detail how national newspapers had 'bought up' relatives and acquaintances of the Yorkshire Ripper Peter Sutcliffe.

To an extent LOP served a readership alienated from the mainstream media. A LOP readers' survey in 1986 found that 35% never read the Evening Post, 65% never read its morning sister the Yorkshire Post, more than 50% never listened to local radio, and between a third and a half never watched the local news programmes on TV.

A few journalists from the mainstream press gave LOP contacts or passed on the occasional story they couldn't use. The process became two-way, as the mainstream press and the broadcast media followed up stories broken by LOP. Many of LOP's paid and unpaid journalists went on to work on mainstream morning and evening newspapers, national magazines, music papers, television, freelance writing and photography, and book publishing. Others went to a variety of jobs, some are on the dole, and a few can today barely bring themselves to open a newspaper or turn on the news.

A Yorkshire Post reporter once told a LOP worker: "It's great when one of you lot turns up at a press conference or council meeting, because nobody knows what you'll ask or print. It keeps them on their toes." There could be a worse epitaph for an alternative paper than that: It kept them on their toes.

Chapter 7

With a Little Help From its Friends

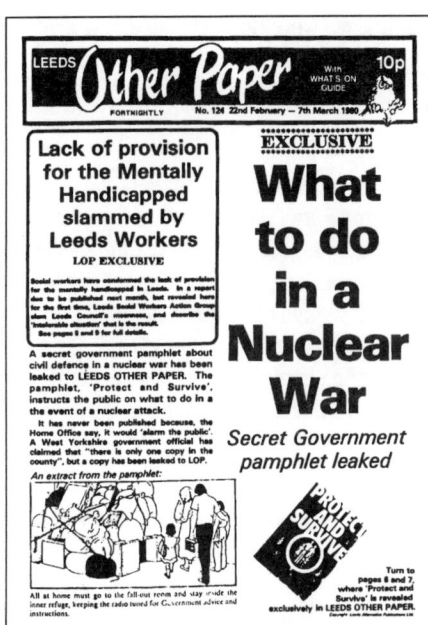

LOP was different from the mainstream press not just in its content, but in its way of working. It had no editor, and anybody offering to help out on the paper was welcome at the editorial meetings where copy was hammered into shape. At least, that was what it was like until production and other pressures gradually took their toll on such participatory democracy. Mat: "The development of the structure was fairly organic. We had an open door policy. If somebody came in and wrote something for the paper, you'd say 'You're welcome to come along to the editorial meeting where it will be discussed'. Everybody read every article and felt free to make a comment on it. We didn't even have a debate about having an editor."

It worked very smoothly when the paper was monthly and fortnightly, with up to around 20 people taking part, but after LOP went weekly the numbers attending the evening editorial meetings dropped. The overworked paid staff then pushed for the meetings to be in the daytime, which made it impossible for supporters in full-time work elsewhere to come along. Eventually not even all LOP's paid staff attended - the printing, advertising and typesetting workers kept their heads down while the paid journalist/s decided what went in that week's paper.

From time to time, LOP tried other ways of involving readers. Occasional public meetings were held to discuss the content of the paper in general, or to debate particular topics such as education. It wasn't all one way. Once a disabled group who felt their concerns hadn't been given enough coverage turned up en masse, switched the press off and wouldn't leave until issues had been thrashed out at a meeting with LOP staff. Another time, a group of NALGO shop stewards took exception to an article which quoted a Children's Rights Officer criticising staff at children's homes. They unsuccessfully tried to get the huge Leeds City Council NALGO branch to boycott the paper. More often, readers on the far right made threatening phone calls, smashed the odd window, and carried out the occasional assault. It was an occupational hazard.

Throughout its life LOP relied on unpaid labour. Alice Nutter, who spent a year on the paid staff, recalls how she started writing for the paper. "I did a spoof review of an anti-fascist band that didn't exist but which I thought ought to exist. They said they couldn't use it, but asked me if I'd like to write anything else. It really encouraged people to write. Without it I never would have written for a paper."

Mat feels that having unpaid journalists helped LOP get its teeth into issues deeper than did the mainstream press. "I was doing a bit of teaching and a bit of electrical re-wiring, but I wasn't working full-time, which meant I could go out and spend time on researching articles. Because it wasn't a job you weren't so worried about spending a lot of time on it. I remember doing detailed articles about tower blocks falling down, for example, and having time to find out who the architect was, making an appointment and interviewing the architect at leisure, talking to one or two other experts, and actually understanding the subject I was writing about - rather than grabbing a few quick quotes over the phone."

LOP didn't just attract frustrated writers in search of an outlet. There were photographers, cartoonists, occasional crossword compilers and countless volunteers who helped paste-up, proof-read, fold, and deliver the paper. John Quayle's Big Doylem cartoon strip, Terry Wragg's Our Lily, Sue Beasley's Co-Op Capers, plus cartoons by Janis Goodman, Boff and numerous others gave some light relief to the frequently depressing news content. And photographers such as Tony Woolgar, Paul Breslin and many others put in countless hours of unpaid time to improve the paper's visual impact.

Ben Denning was unemployed when, in 1983, he responded to a blurb in LOP asking for people to get involved. He stayed for a decade. "At first I was only doing an hour a week, helping proof-read the What's On guide," he recalls. "Then I started doing the plate-making and working on photos trying to get cracks to show up - there were always loads of damp stories and pictures of people pointing to cracks in their houses."

Ben went on to become a paid production worker. "When I started more people seemed to be involved and know what was going on in the paper," he says. "Then over the years it got more and more difficult to produce. It got bigger and more time was spent on printing it and putting it together and less time was spent on other stuff. The pressure of producing it became more important than the content."

While volunteers continued to help with the What's On Guide to the very end, the number of unpaid contributors to the news section got fewer and fewer. The numbers had declined by the late 1980s when that was transformed into policy. Quintin: "One of the things I wanted to do in the news section was to get rid of anything that wasn't written by staff or very good volunteers. No campaign group was allowed to write. We really upset people, like we refused to take anything from Nicaragua Solidarity and they were just shouting down the phone. It was a deliberate policy, to get rid of all foreign coverage because we couldn't do it properly, and to get rid of anything that wasn't written by somebody who could write, and anything that was overtly political and just supporting one group. I guess that slightly isolated us, but those volunteers took an enormous amount of time."

And time, as they say, is money.

Chapter 8
Eight Days a Week

Contrary to popular belief, there was life before listings. Although details of a few meetings and helpful telephone numbers began creeping in, it wasn't until issue 52 in April 1977 that LOP launched its What's On Guide. A four page pull-out printed on yellow paper, it proclaimed itself 'a fortnightly guide to events and happenings in Leeds'. Listings ranged from punk band Generation X at the Fforde Grene pub to Music for Holy Week at Leeds Parish Church. For the politico around town, the meetings and events column provided no end of attractions: a Chilean Social Evening, a World Revolution debate on China, the launch of a Big Flame manifesto, the inaugural meeting of Energy 2000, plus the regular meetings of the Socialist Women's Action Group, the George Cummings Anarchist Association, Leeds Campaign Against the Cuts, and the Campaign Against a Criminal Trespass Law.

For the next five years the What's On Guide changed backwards and forwards between a four page A4 pull-out and a double sided A3 poster. In addition, a few reviews of plays or gigs were thrown in at the back of what was known as the 'main paper'. March 1982 saw listings, previews, reviews and related display advertising combined in an expanded guide covering pages 12 to 19 of the 20 page paper (40%). The What's On continued to expand, and by the early editions of Northern Star in 1991 it covered pages 11 to 27 of a 28 page paper (60%), and its last few issues three years later devoted pages 7 to 23 of a 24 page paper to What's On material (74%). It boasted 'over 600 listings, eight days a week'.

But the figures only tell part of the story. When LOP launched its What's On Guide, it was almost a new thing. London had Time Out, but no other city had a comprehensive and frequent listings service covering cinema, different types of music, exhibitions and so on. By the 1990s most local, regional and national newspapers had their own listings.

There was, however, a difference in emphasis. LOP's What's On Guide was more likely to give prominence to a play at a community centre than to a Hollywood blockbuster at the Odeon. A Rock Against Racism gig with a local band was regarded as more important than the Rolling Stones at Roundhay Park. For small and occasional venues and community promoters who didn't get a look in with the mainstream press, LOP was a lifeline. It enabled them to reach a sympathetic audience looking for somewhere to go. Listings, previews and reviews were, on the whole, written for love by well-informed enthusiasts. The paper even had its own idiosyncratic Rugby League column written by Ludwig Kasatkin from Castleford (or Lagentium).

From 1987 until the end the guide included a gay and lesbian page called 'Out In The North' which developed from a noticeboard for events to an open forum for debate within the gay and lesbian communities in Leeds. A remarkable achievement for a non-specifically-gay publication.

Over the years different companies launched commercial What's On Guides in Leeds in a bid to profit from the market partially identified by LOP- but none lasted long. Ben: "None of the What's On papers that started in Leeds have ever been as good. Live music, small theatre groups and cabaret got coverage that they wouldn't have anywhere else. All you can do now is flypost, or leave leaflets in places that people don't go to anymore."

According to Alice, who went on to contribute a frank sex column and now dresses up as a nun to sing with Leeds band Chumbawamba, the demise of LOP/Northern Star's What's On Guide has left a 'massive' gap in the city's culture. "There's no What's On guide that is willing to cover things that otherwise you'd never hear about, from poetry to jazz to indi-pop to grunge to theatre. There's nothing that brings everything together."

Over its second decade there were frequent debates among LOP workers about whether people bought the paper for the news or the listings. LOP's home-made attempts at market research failed to provide a definitive answer, probably because different people bought it for different reasons at different times. Results from readers' surveys in the What's On Guide's early years suggested that 75% of readers used the guide to plan their nights out, and 76% said they liked the guide compared to 51% who said they liked the paper's news coverage. By 1992, when a street survey was carried out, of 95 readers asked what section of the paper they read first, just 17 said news or features while 71 said What's On.

Julie: "One of LOP's successes was that it started the What's On guide as an information resource, and it kept it going and fought off all-comers, mainly because we were weekly. But I think there was a gradual change over the years from being a newspaper which provided a What's On service to its news readers, to where it was largely What's On and the news became secondary."

According to Alice: "When I started writing I wanted to mix politics and culture. I think it went too far later. It became the paper with an actor on the cover."

Chapter 9

Desperately Seeking Readers

It was depressing. A random street survey in 1992 discovered that 62% of those questioned had never even heard of Northern Star or Leeds Other Paper. That was almost precisely the same figure as hadn't heard of LOP during a similar exercise in the late 1970s. Perhaps it wasn't so surprising. Even well-established papers like the Yorkshire Evening Post feel the need to advertise their existence, yet LOP never had any money for advertising. Apart from occasional flyposting forays, the paper's sole attempt at advertising was a cinema commercial. Costing less than £100, it featured a selection of LOP workers and supporters reading the paper in a variety of situations. It was screened at the Hyde Park Picture House in Leeds and the Bradford Film Theatre, in exchange for their adverts in LOP. Sales didn't noticeably soar as a result.

In fact, sales of the paper never dramatically changed. They stayed stubbornly around the 2,000 figure for almost its entire 20 year existence. It was a quest for the missing readers that prompted the changes of the last few years: increasing the size of the What's On Guide, introducing more features on 'popular' issues, downgrading the news, and changing the name from Leeds Other Paper to Northern Star in the vain hope of selling more outside Leeds. In fact it sold less in Leeds without picking up many readers outside. "A year later old readers were still saying 'I used to buy LOP but I can never find it now'," recalls Ben.

With half an eye on the increasing numbers of glossy mags on newsagents' shelves, more time was spent designing the paper, Paula Solloway was recruited as a paid photographer, and the cover started featuring a large picture aimed at attracting the casual shopper's attention, especially the younger ones. Quintin: "Our analysis was that we had a declining market. LOP readers who were 40 were dying off and we needed a new growth base." Alice adds: "It was desperate. You wanted to get readers in without selling your soul. We did keep trying new things. What it needed was a massive cash injection."

But there wasn't a massive cash injection, and in a bid to win new readers the paper had more and more features about 'popular culture', largely sex, rock bands and TV. Like many first and second generation Loppers, Julie is critical of much of the later content, but she's not sure whether there was much alternative. "What would have happened if they hadn't done it? I just wonder whether things would have carried on going downhill increasingly rapidly, and they'd have ended up hardly selling any at all. There isn't the sort of buoyant level of political activity going on in the city to provide a backbone for it."

The Leeds of today is very different from the 'gritty' city of Alan Bennett, Keith Waterhouse, Don Revie and the early LOP. The engineering, textiles and mining industries have been decimated, to be replaced by a city of shopping and financial services. In the mid-1970s just one issue of LOP would feature more strikes and community actions than the city might see in a whole year by the 1990s. But things were still going on even if not so many people were looking for them. Some changes in the content of LOP were inevitable, but Quintin accepts that a lot of old readers were lost in the early 'nineties: "I got fed up with what they wanted. For some of them it was just a reminder of their youth, they wanted something that was constantly there and constantly radical, no matter what they were doing now and what the reality was."

For many 'old-timers' (as they were regarded by the last wave of Northern Star workers), it had been a mistake for the paper to lose touch with its former political base. Gordon: "When LOP became Northern Star there was this conscious policy switch to embrace what I was told was popular culture, but I thought they were embracing a very narrow view of culture which meant interviewing your local rock group. We had been fiercely independent, and we'd had quite a few rows with other people on the left, but basically people would rally round and support us and recognise us as part of the left-wing community. With those changes I think it lost that. It was partly to do with a conscious decision of the paper, but a bit of me says it's mirrored the way society has gone, and the left has disintegrated in Leeds to a large extent. So perhaps it might have happened anyway."

Chapter 10

Money's Too Tight to Mention

The boatyard in East Anglia had been staked out by the police. Fraud squad officers were lying in wait for Robert, who duly arrived to hire a boat in the name of Leeds Alternative Publications. Robert was the finance manager at LOP and he'd done a runner.

It was 1991 and LOP workers were pleased to have appointed the quietly spoken financial wizard who was keen on computerising the co-op's accounts. The co-op had just made its first ever trading profit, and money had been raised to secure the paper's future by investing in desktop publishing equipment. Robert had kidney trouble, and every now and then he would disappear for time-consuming dialysis treatment at St James' Hospital in Leeds. Or so his colleagues were told.

It was while he was off sick that alarm bells began ringing, when a leasing company which had supplied some equipment said the paperwork had been wrongly filled in. Robert had taken some of the equipment home to set up before bringing it into the office. He was off sick when the company contacted LOP, so Mat and Quintin called at his house. Neighbours said he was at St James' undergoing dialysis, but when Mat and Quintin went to the hospital they discovered there was no record of any patient of that name.

Mat: "We went back the next day and talked to a neighbour who said he'd gone to Ireland. We went back again and found someone in his house who was a mate of his and we said 'Can we look round?' The computer equipment wasn't there. Another neighbour accused us of acting like Starsky and Hutch. Quintin went back again later and got the keys, went in and found a copy of Exchange and Mart open at the page of second hand computers for sale with certain numbers ringed, and also a boatyard in East Anglia ringed. So I said 'Let's get the cops in'.

"Robert had been buying stuff with LOP money and flogging it, he'd pinched petty cash, he'd booked hotels in Scotland under the name Leeds Alternative Publications. I reckon he got about £10,000, which wiped out the benefits we'd made over the previous two years. Bad news always seemed to follow good. It put us back to square one, with everybody feeling demoralised and frustrated that this leap to new technology was knocked on the head."

Having been arrested in East Anglia, Robert was eventually convicted and given community service. But the money was never recovered.

It had been a bitter blow for an organisation balanced on a financial knife-edge and reliant on trust. Since the workers' co-op was formed and some people began being paid in the 1970s, LOP had survived on income from sales, advertising, typesetting and, after the move to Cookridge Street, commercial printing. It had only survived at all because of unpaid and underpaid labour and an overworked staff.

Despite the early use of Job Creation Scheme money and small grants for equipment from Leeds City Council and the Rowntree Trust, LOP always needed to generate its own income. Sometimes it worked. Mat: "As a commercial enterprise, when we first got the typesetting equipment and the press, the general financial situation of the co-op was relatively healthy. Union branches had money and were quite happy to pay for a trade union recognised print shop. But the amount of printwork that we did and the profitability of that work suddenly took a nosedive. For most of the co-op's time there was very little financial management."

Things weren't helped by having to move out of Cookridge Street in 1987 to make way for redevelopment of the building (which is today the Town and Country Club). LOP moved first to a corner of a rat-infested former warehouse on The Calls, and six months later to a former porn cinema on Call Lane. "The low point was when we moved into Call Lane, we had a clapped out press, we'd been losing money for a number of years, we'd accumulated debts, and we had an underpaid and demoralised workforce," explains Mat.

The paper was rescued then by Mat and a few others organising a major fund-raising appeal combined with Common Ownership Securities - a sort of alternative share issue which raised capital while retaining control within the co-op. Enough readers responded to raise a total of £7,510 in 'securities'; most of them realised they were never likely to see that money again. Benefits and donations brought in more money, but an attempt at persuading national celebrities to send a few quid was singularly unsuccessful. LOP even wrote to self-proclaimed socialist millionaire Robert Maxwell to ask for a donation. To everyone's amusement, Captain Bob wrote back personally to decline, adding: "You will appreciate that the Mirror Group and Maxwell Communication Corporation make heavy demands on my time, and I am not prepared to make investments to which I can not devote proper attention." Phew!

Although there was a temporary resurgence in the co-op's fortunes when a new printer arrived from a Welsh co-op that had gone bust, bringing better equipment with him, the proceeds were removed by Robert the finance manager before LOP could derive any long-term benefit. Money got tighter, wages were paid late and sometimes never, staff turnover increased, and as the 1990s wore on it became harder to get anyone at all prepared to work at LOP on wages of £72 gross for a supposedly three-day-week. While many first and second generation Loppers stayed around for a decade, in the 1990s workers were more likely to leave after months rather than years. Ben: "It turned into a drudge. By the time it finished there didn't seem any point to it in terms of news. When it came down to it, the only point of working in such bad conditions for little or sometimes no pay was to do different news. You wouldn't do that for a What's On Guide or a printshop."

If financial problems were endemic, the final crisis which pushed it over the edge wasn't much more serious than previous ones that had been survived. The liquidator's report reveals that when the paper went bust it had assets of £9,000 and owed over £40,000. But more than £15,000 of that was either money loaned by Mat over the years or else it came in with the Common Ownership Securities: it wasn't exactly being demanded with menaces.

Geraldine recalls the last few days at Northern Star. "We couldn't afford to take anyone on, and everyone was doing other people's jobs to a really ridiculous extent. Then the paper suppliers stopped supplying us with paper."

LOP had exhausted its credit with numerous paper suppliers, and the remaining workers decided to call it a day. There was no longer a large and active support group on hand to rescue the paper with more fund-raising efforts. Whether readers would have responded to another appeal isn't known, because Northern Star closed without warning. There was just enough paper in the building to print the final issue, number 820, dated 20 January 1994, and then the receivers were called in. It was 20 years to the day since the paper began. The printer demanded payment in cash upfront before he would print the final issue. It was not a happy ending.

Chapter 11
One Step Beyond

"The co-op is heading for a serious crisis in the near future for three interrelated reasons: lack of financial documentation, control or planning, combined with falling circulation and advertising, and a lack of clarity about the future direction of the organisation." Written in 1992 by a post-graduate student for a thesis on LOP/Northern Star, those words could have described most if not all periods during the previous decade or so.

The paper eventually fell victim to the political and economic forces that had already killed off most other alternative papers. Was its death inevitable? Probably not, but it was always possible and often probable. Keith: "The waves made in 1968 rippled right through for 15 years of LOP or more, but the carpet was pulled from under it politically. It's very difficult to just say this is where it went wrong. We all know what 15 years of Thatcherism has done to things like education, health services and God knows what. Well, poor little Leeds Other Paper struggled a long time."

According to Quintin: "In 1991 or 1992 when Thatcher's children actually grew up, that was it. Suddenly there was this barren desert out there and you were lucky if you could get anybody with a slice of commitment to anything."

As this pamphlet went to press in the Summer of 1994 there was talk of a group in the Belle Isle area of Leeds reviving the title Northern Star. It remains to be seen if it will happen, and if so in what form. Some people doubt if there is any future for alternative newspapers at all, and suggest that more hope lies in electronic media such as pirate radio, community radio, cable TV or even electronic mail networks. But the printed word is not yet dead, and desktop publishing today offers more possibilities than were available when LOP was launched in 1974. The growth of football and music fanzines in recent years suggests that alternatives can be published where there is both the commitment and a defined market.

From my personal experience at LOP, mixed with hindsight, I believe that any group in Leeds or elsewhere thinking of starting an alternative newspaper should decide who it is aimed at and how the paper is going to reach them. Other points to be considered (some of which we tried at LOP at different times) include:

- An alternative paper should be self-disciplined enough to avoid the content becoming boring or dominated by particular hobby-horses;
- Those involved should make the time to study the law on libel and contempt to avoid possibly costly mistakes;
- The paper should have structures that allow maximum participation of those producing the paper;
- It should aim to involve the readers in a two-way process;
- An alternative paper should not lightly abandon existing readers in the hope of attracting mythical new ones;
- Even when everyone has got their heads down working like the clappers, it should be somebody's specific job to take volunteer would-be journalists under their wing, to train and nurture them, and to thereby increase rather than decrease the paper's role as a news service and journal of investigation;
- Organisations such as trade unions and the voluntary sector who would benefit from the existence of such an independent paper, even though they might not always agree with every word printed, should consider putting some money where their mouths are by supporting the alternative press financially through donations, levies, bulk buying, or regular advertising.

Of the need for some alternative there is little doubt, even though Quintin believes "the alternative press changed the established press, it forced it to start reporting community groups and all the rest of it". The national press is dominated by Rupert Murdoch and the Mirror Group, major cities no longer have a choice of evening paper, local weekly papers are usually owned by the same group, and the Government's relaxation of cross-media ownership restrictions means that the major newspaper publishing groups are soon likely to control large chunks of commercial TV and radio too. The newspaper industry has been at the forefront of undermining trade unions, a process which has done nothing to increase readers' choice or to raise standards.

In their 1991 study of the local press, Bob Franklin and David Murphy suggested there were hardly any traditional local papers left at all, since most local independent publishers had been taken over by giant conglomerates. They wrote: "The localism of the local press is increasingly illusory; the market, ownership, the political system and cultural influences such as notions of style are increasingly homogenised and centralised. There is in prospect no visible countervailing tendency which would suggest a reinvigoration of the local press as a means of scrutinising or informing a system of local politics which has been stifled and undermined."

Franklin and Murphy went on to suggest some worthy measures to improve the situation: "a fund established to support local newspapers offering an alternative to the existing bill of fare; restrictions on monopoly ownership of the local press; guaranteed working conditions and rights for journalists (not least to belong to a trade union); and the establishment of a critical watchdog press council, funded from sources other than the Newspaper Society, with a specific brief to monitor the quality and journalistic integrity of the local press."

Don't hold your breath. In the here and now, it seems the only hope of an alternative will be if some community activists decide to take up where LOP and its counterparts left off. The alternative press may have been small, but in a world where information is power it was never insignificant. As Julie says: "It was only a grotty little thing produced on a few sheets of recycled paper that 2,000 people would buy, but that doesn't measure up to the impact it had over the years. It had a profound effect on Leeds in its small way."

"...we sincerely hope that it won't be too long before someone else organises a publication which can continue the job we started 20 years ago."
(Northern Star 820, January 1994.)